Peggy Parrish
27916 Klahr Rd
Parma, Idaho 83660
teacuplady53.blogspot.com
Copy picture artwork by Peggy Parrish
Inside artwork designed by Peggy Parrish

ISBN-13 978-1530581429
ISBN-10 1530581427
Printed in the United States of America
First Edition March 2016

THE BANDANA CLOTHESLINE

Written and Designed by
Peggy Parrish

"A How to Color Bandana Book"
BANDANA WORKS

Bandana Color Up Tips

1. Markers with small tips work well for small areas of bandana. If markers are used, place a scrap paper under your work so the marker won't leak on another page.

2. Colored pencils work well. My favorite are Prisma. Watercolor pencils work nicely. But any colored pencil is adequate.

3. You may make a few copies for your own use or at home. You may want to put colored by and your own name on the ones you are proud of.

4. Watch for other Bandana Works Adult Coloring Books as they come out.
ENJOY!

MORE TIPS

Bandana Coloring works best if you color one color up to the design and stop.(stop and jump) Leave the design white at first. When all the background has been colored you can choose to color in the design work with another color, black or leave it white. The combinations are nearly endless. That is the fun of this book. You can make an entirely different looking wardrobe from others coloring this book. If you want to make an extra copy or two and experiment with stronger paper, laminating and putting embellishments on your favorites then go for it. Bandana coloring takes only a few techniques to be quite beautiful and unique.

*This is a SPECIAL TIP I discovered. If you want some part of your clothes drawings to look like denim use the bottom of an ordinary blue crayon.

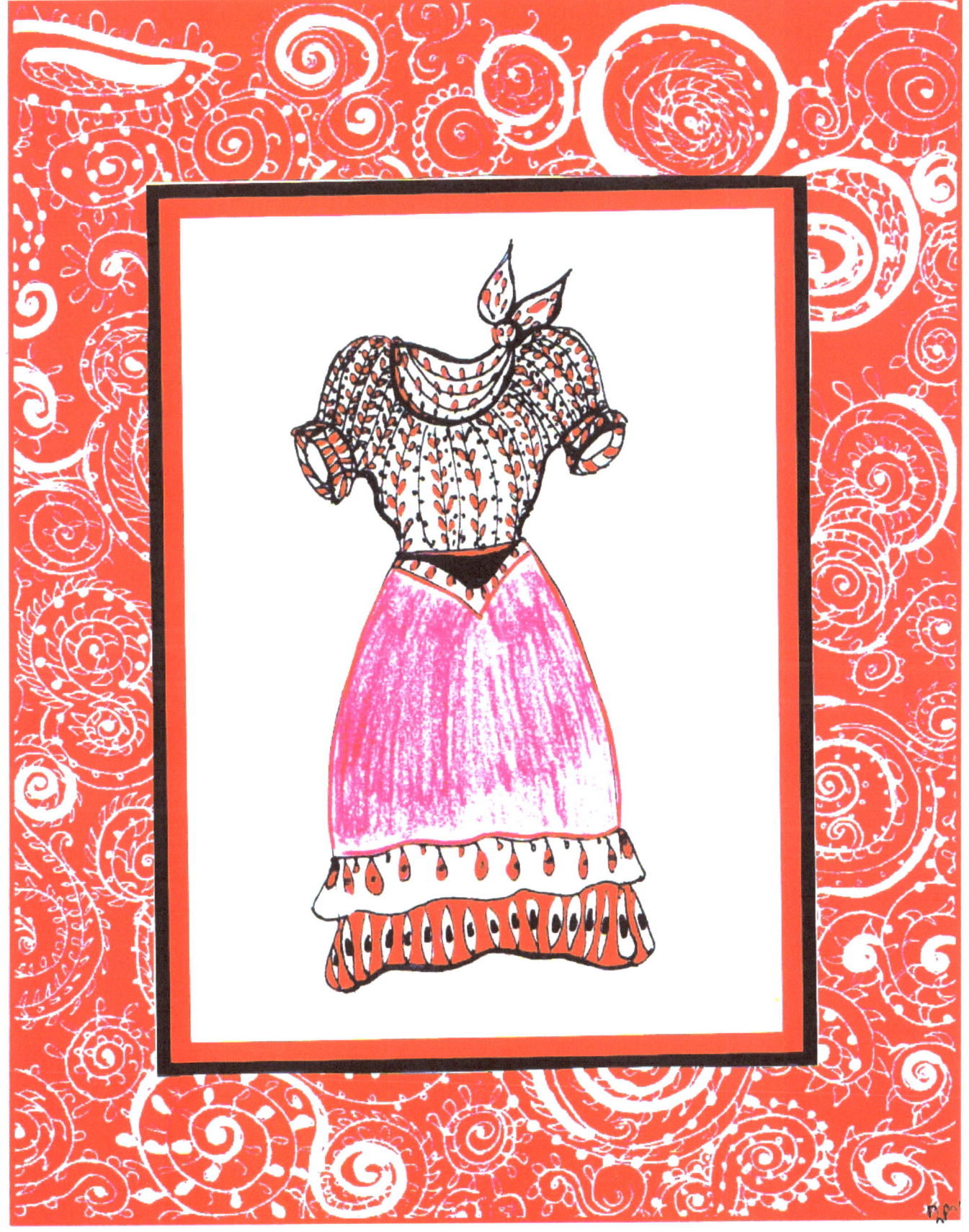

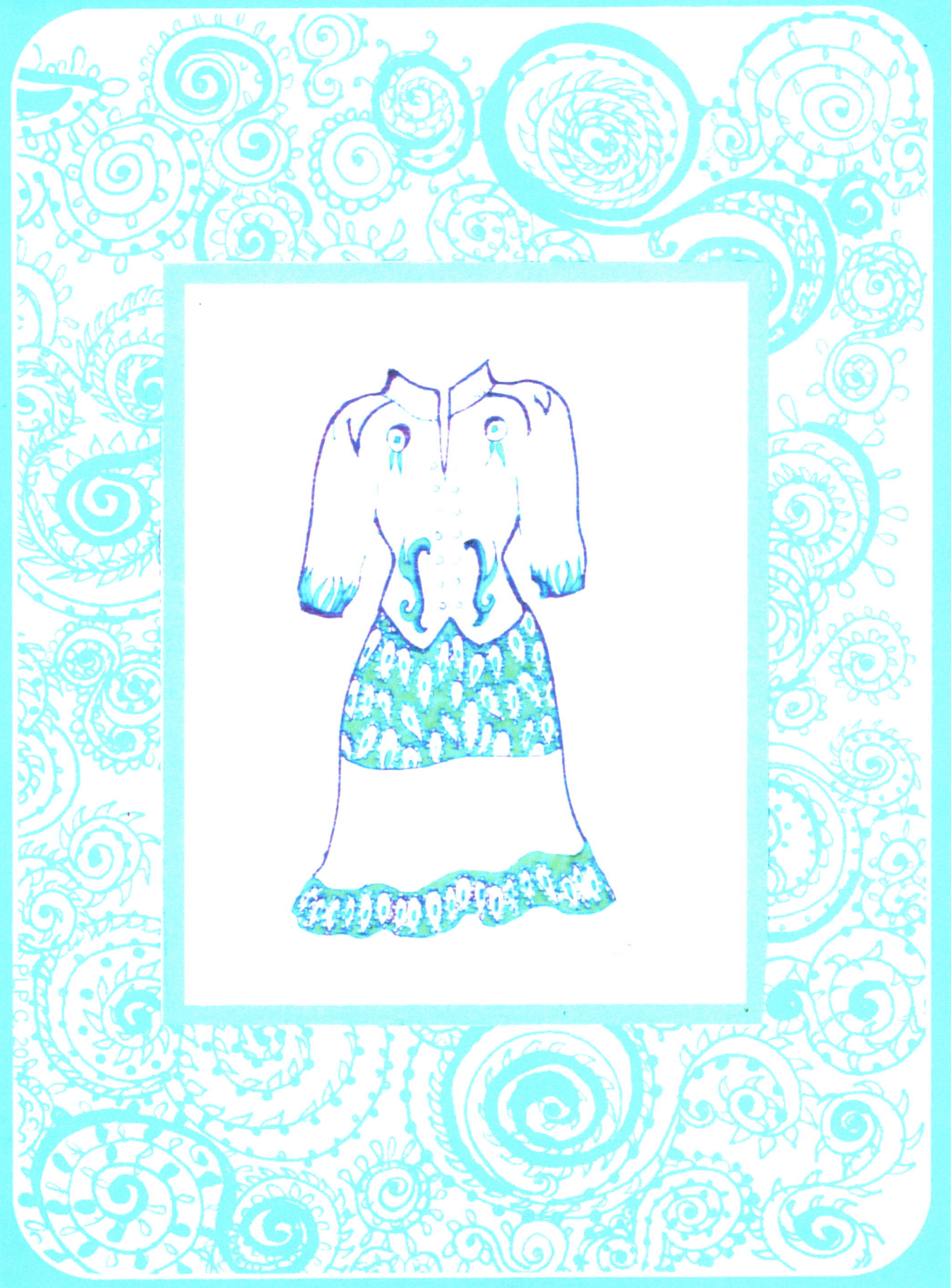

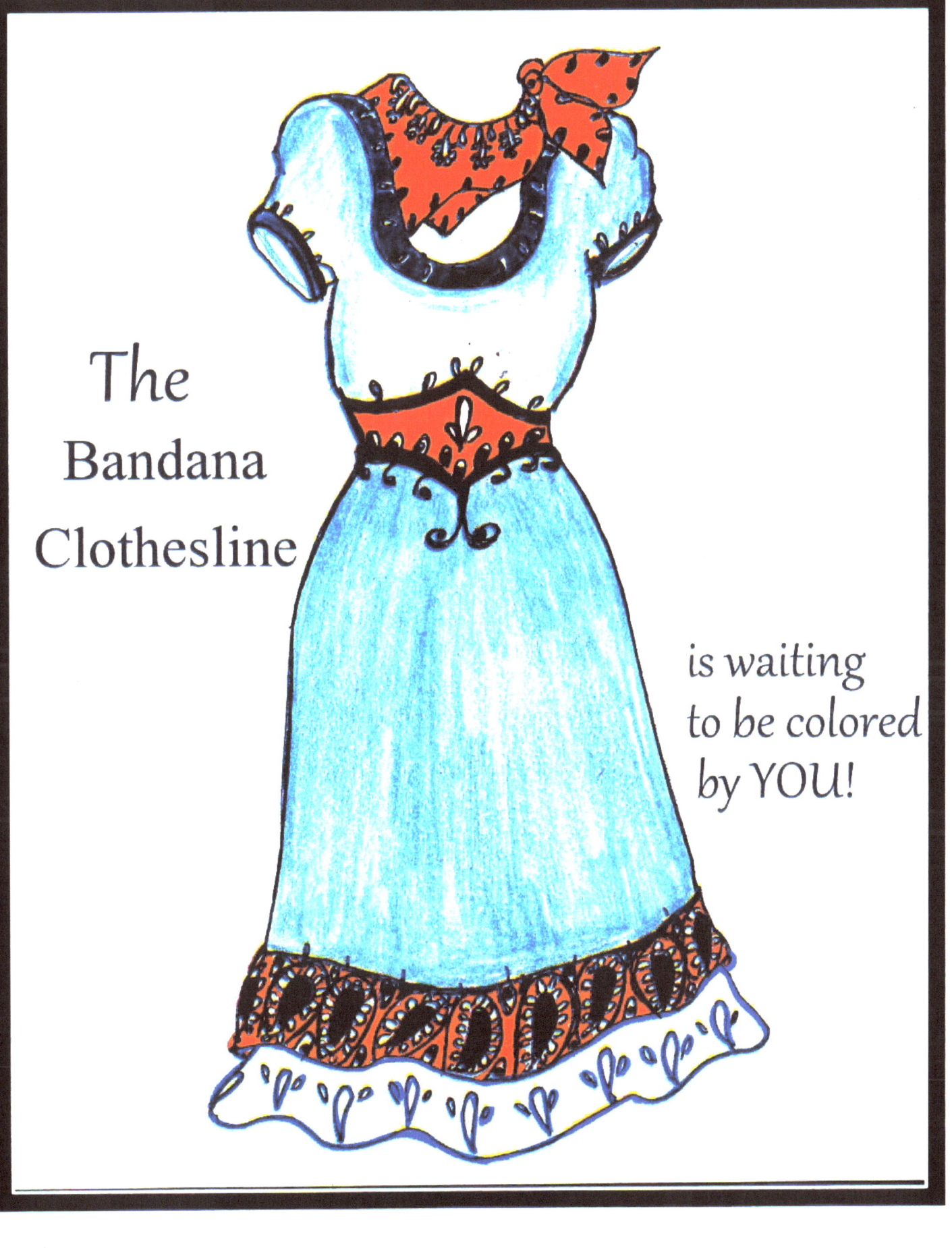

The
Bandana
Clothesline

is waiting
to be colored
by YOU!

So Sweet Bandany

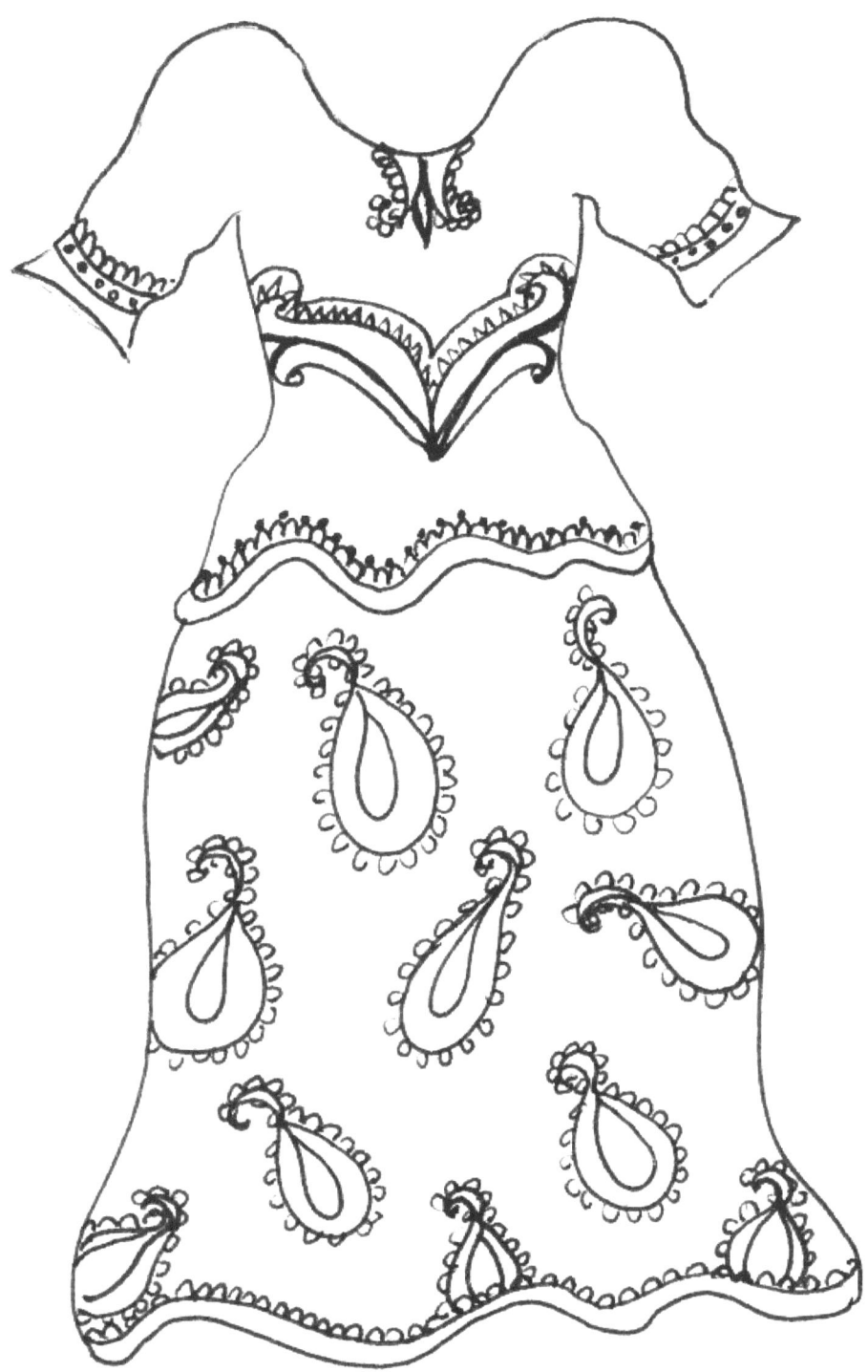

Tourist Tease

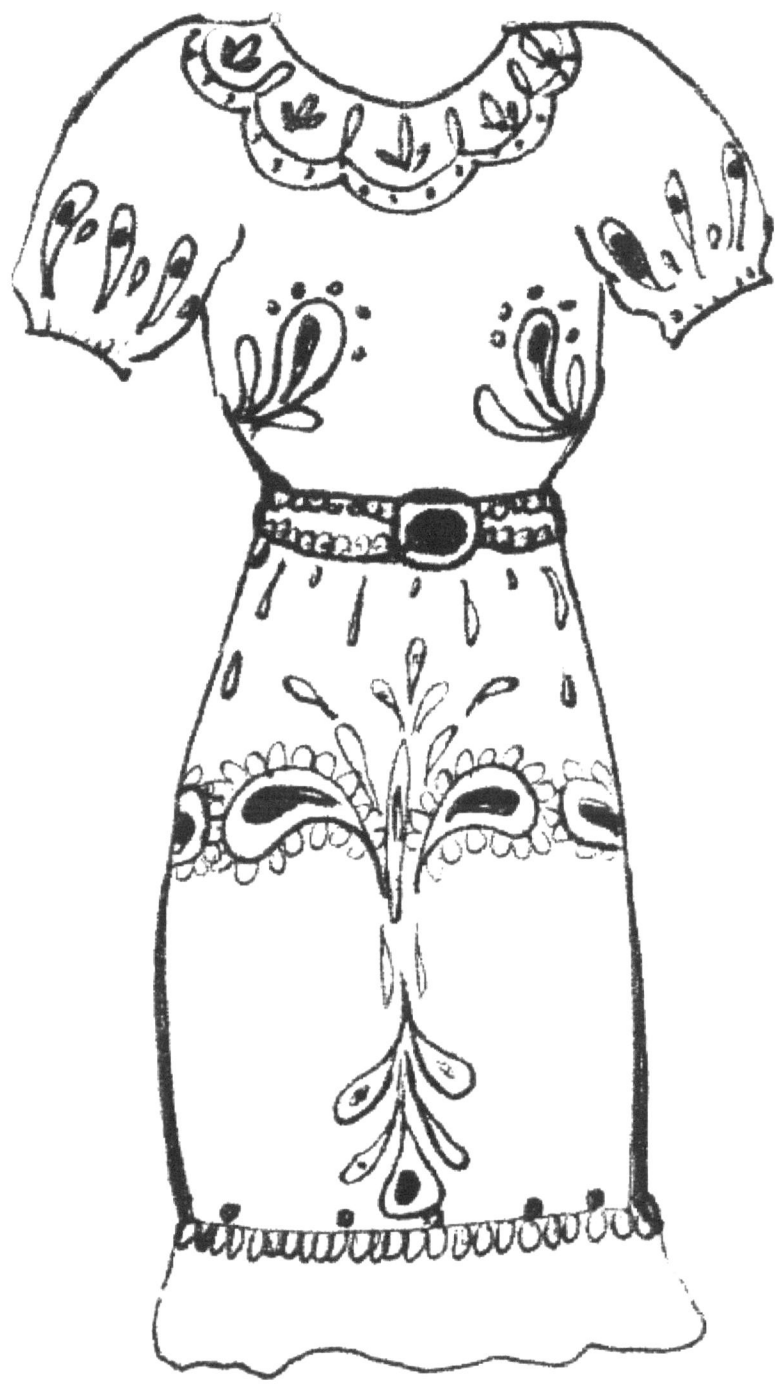

Summer Heartstruck

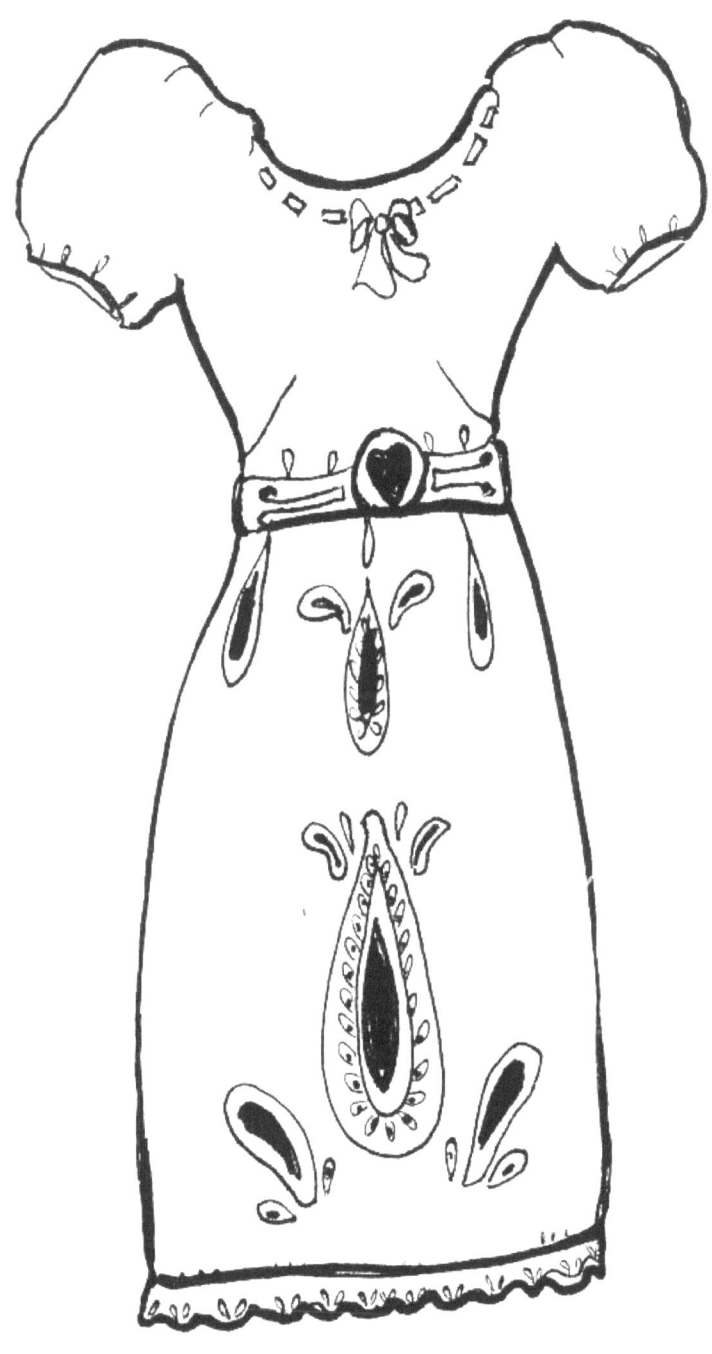

The Altogether

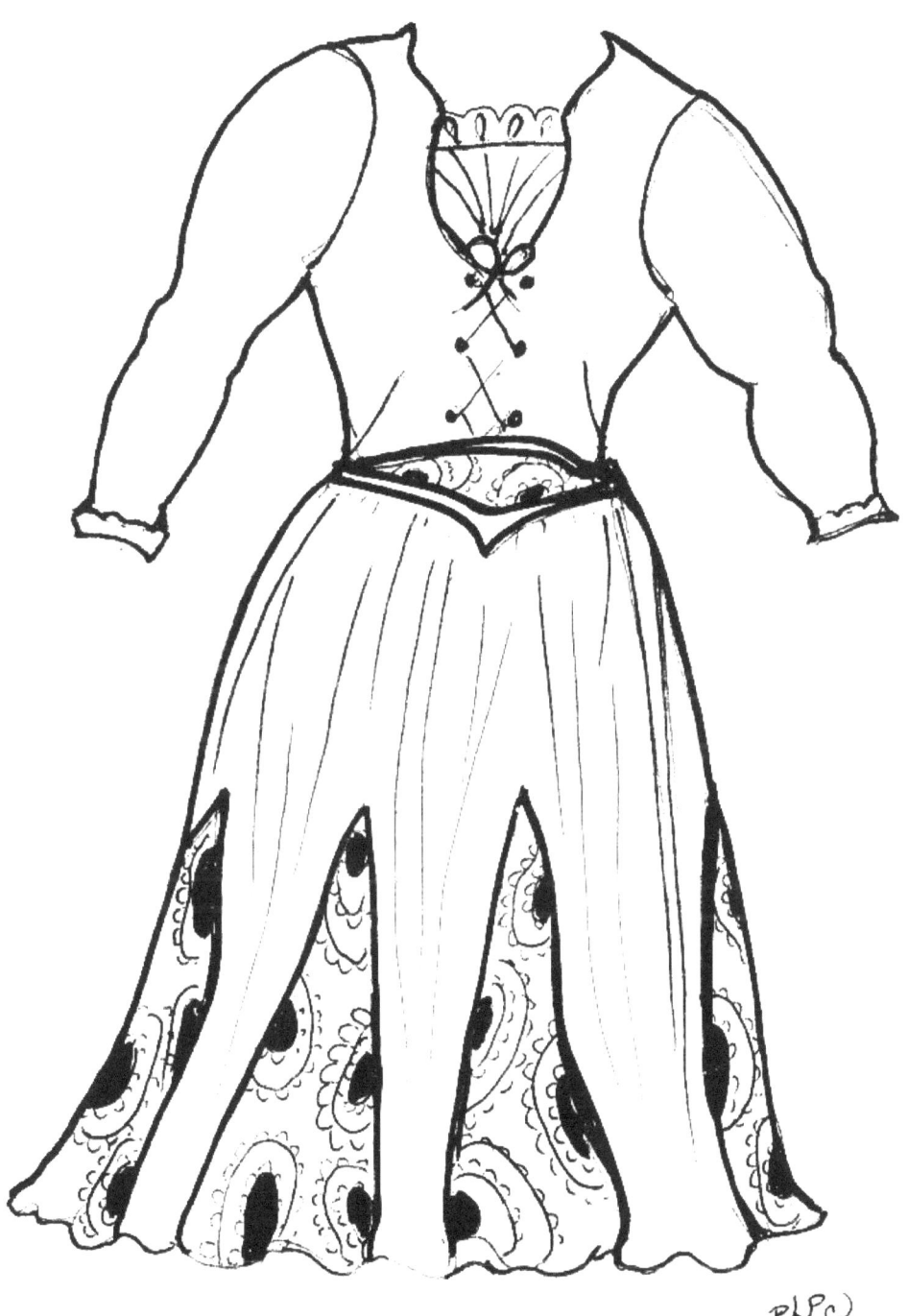

Classy Bandany

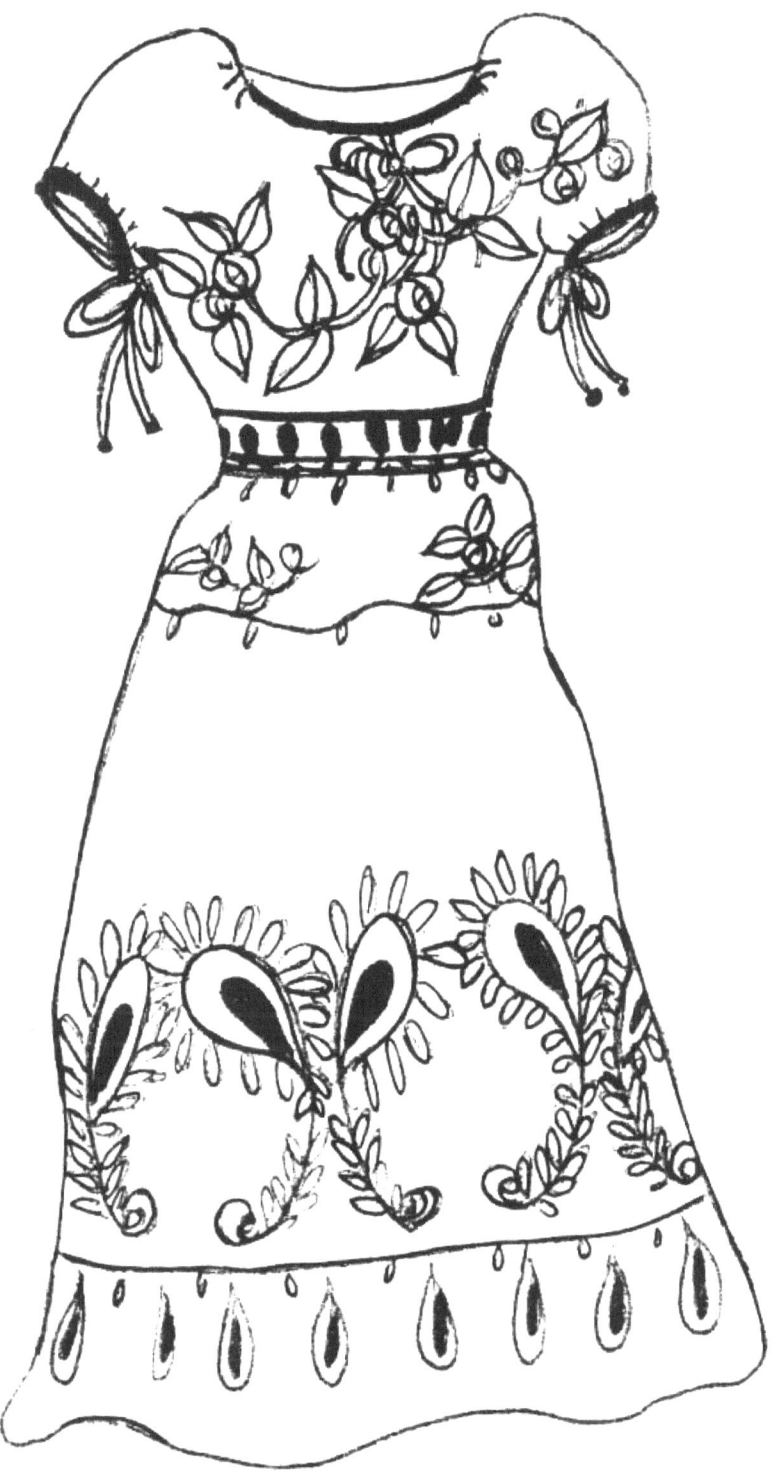

Old World

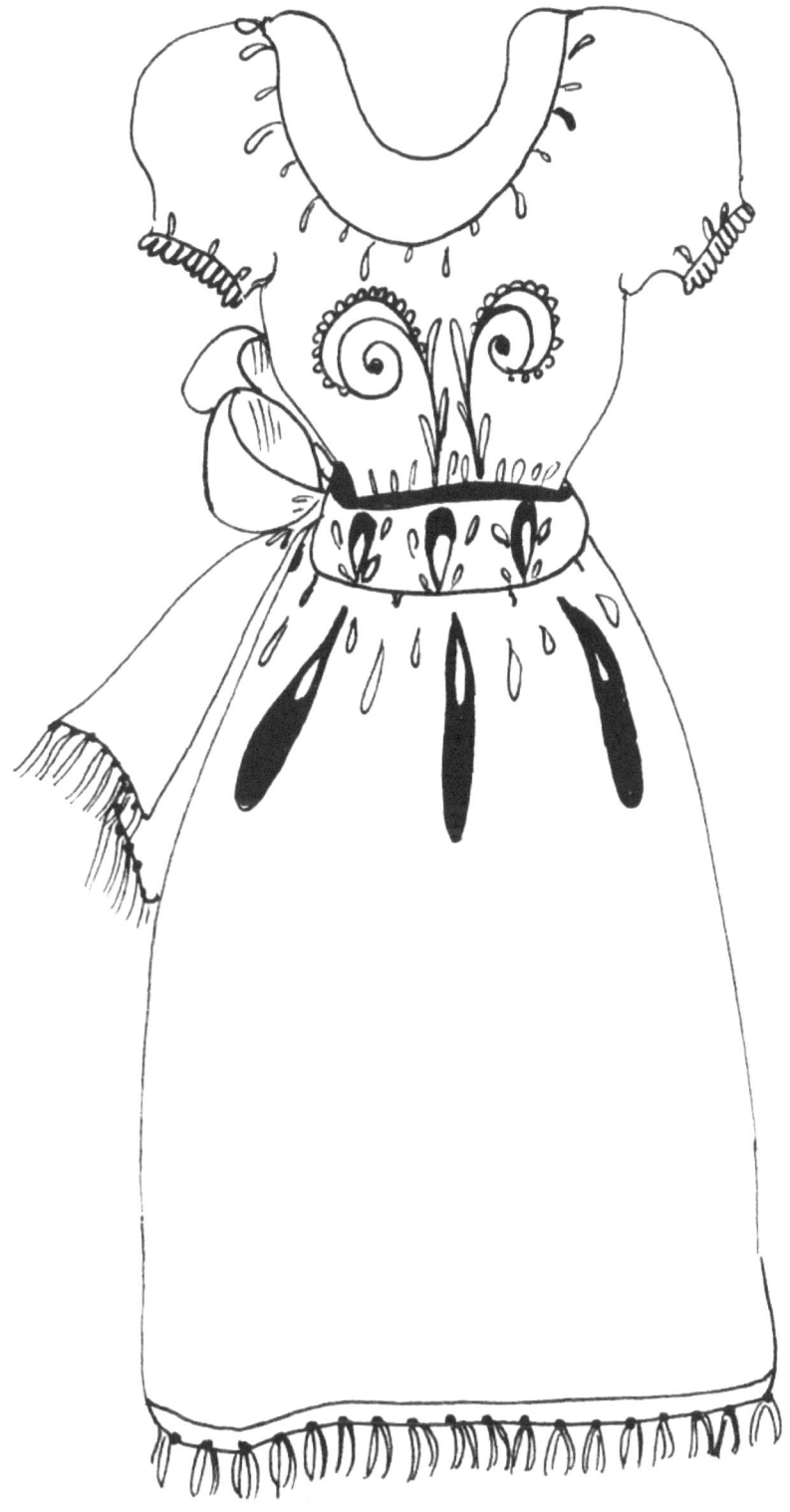

Bandany Tea Time

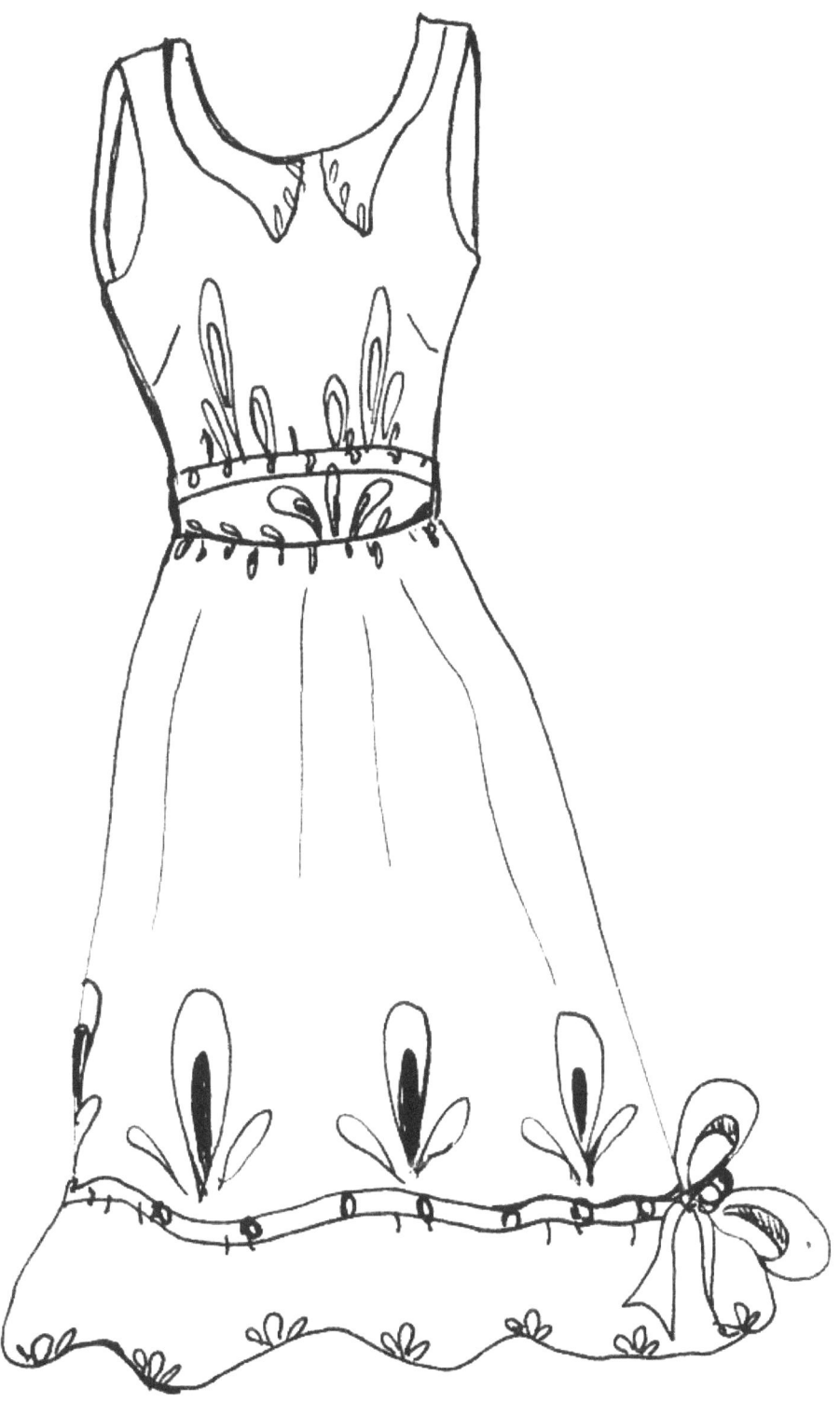

Bandany Rose

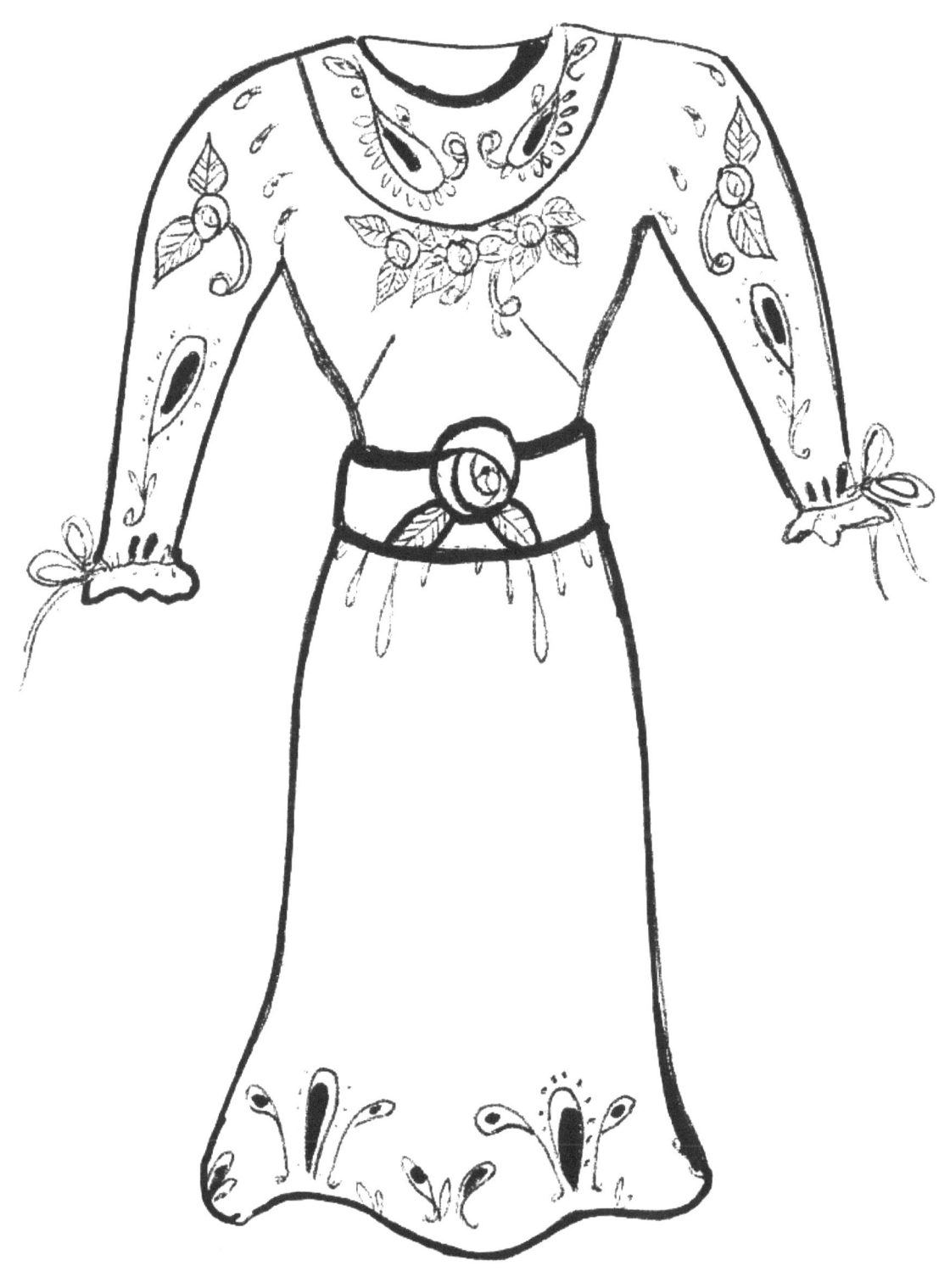

Western Wonder

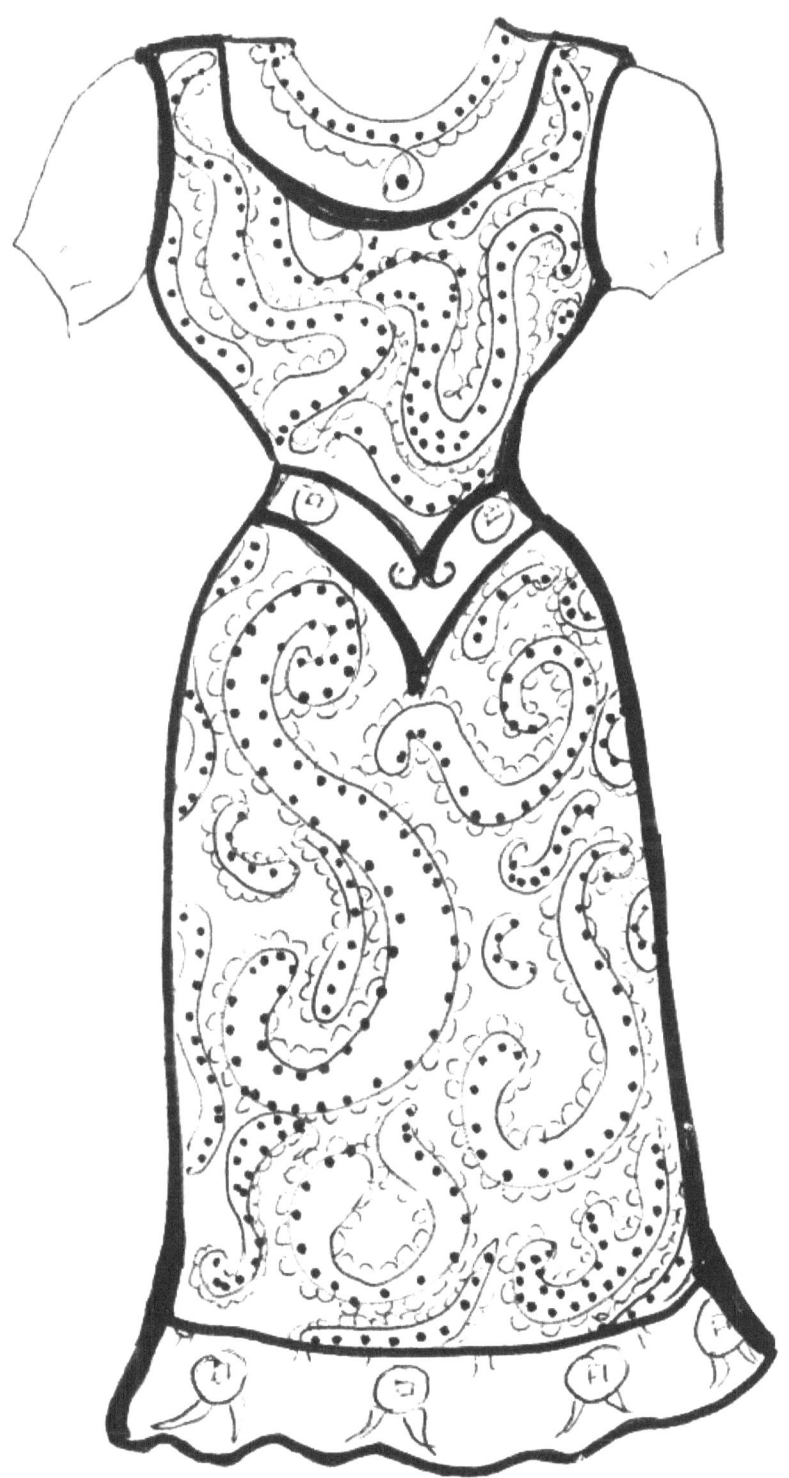

Glorious Night

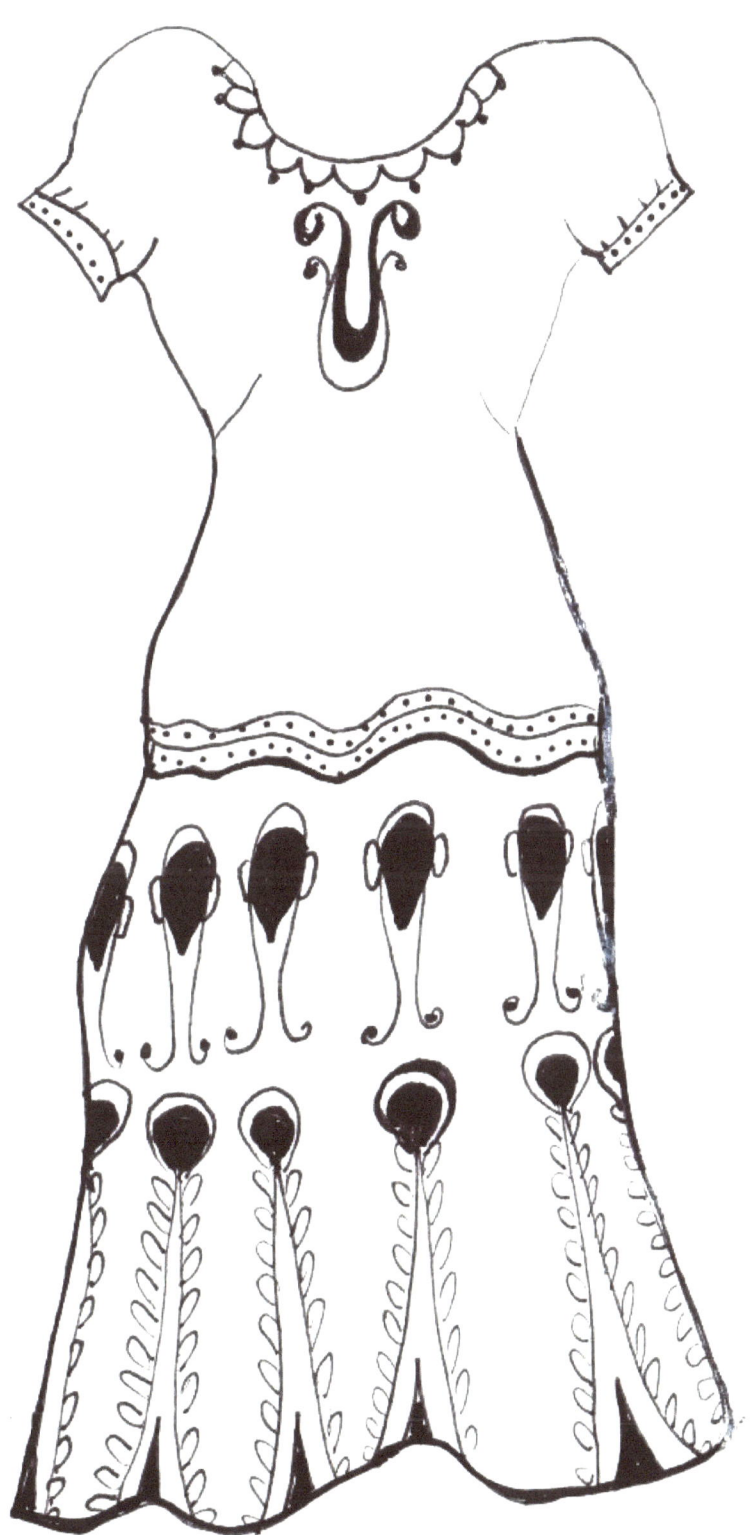

Western Best

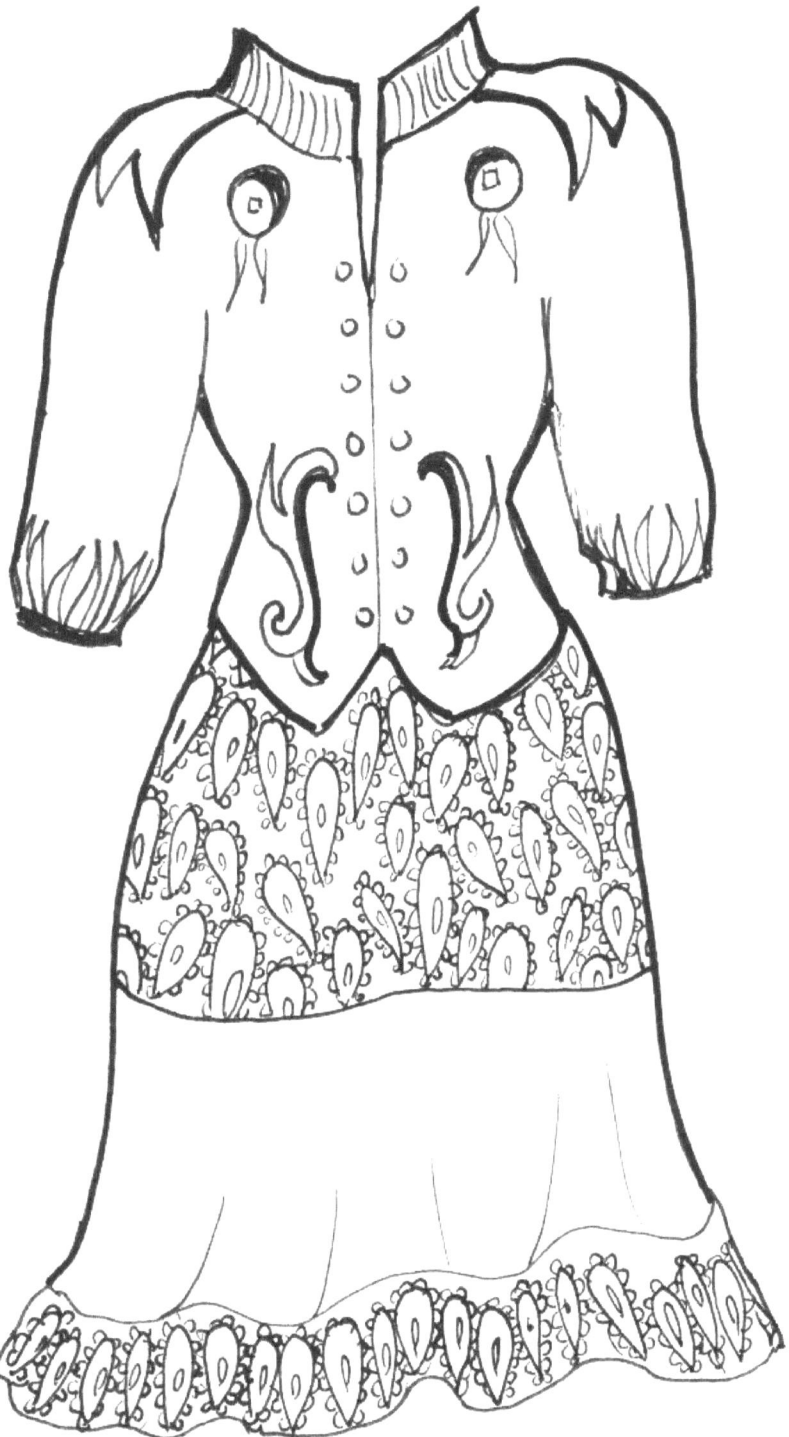

On The Go Cowgirl

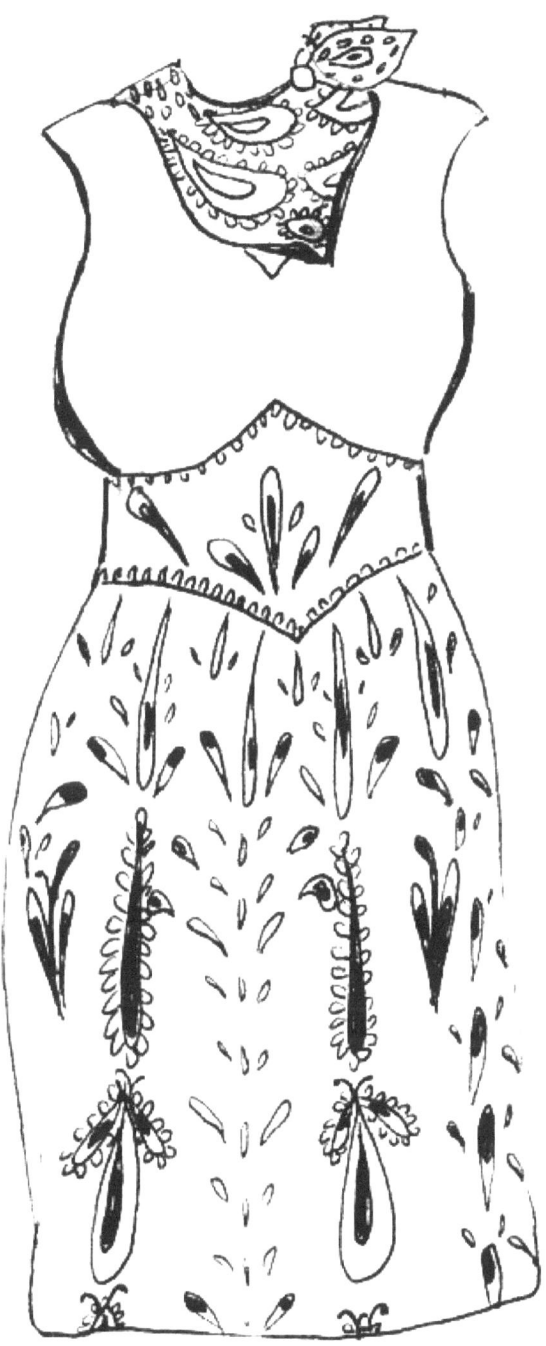

Bandany Heart Wear

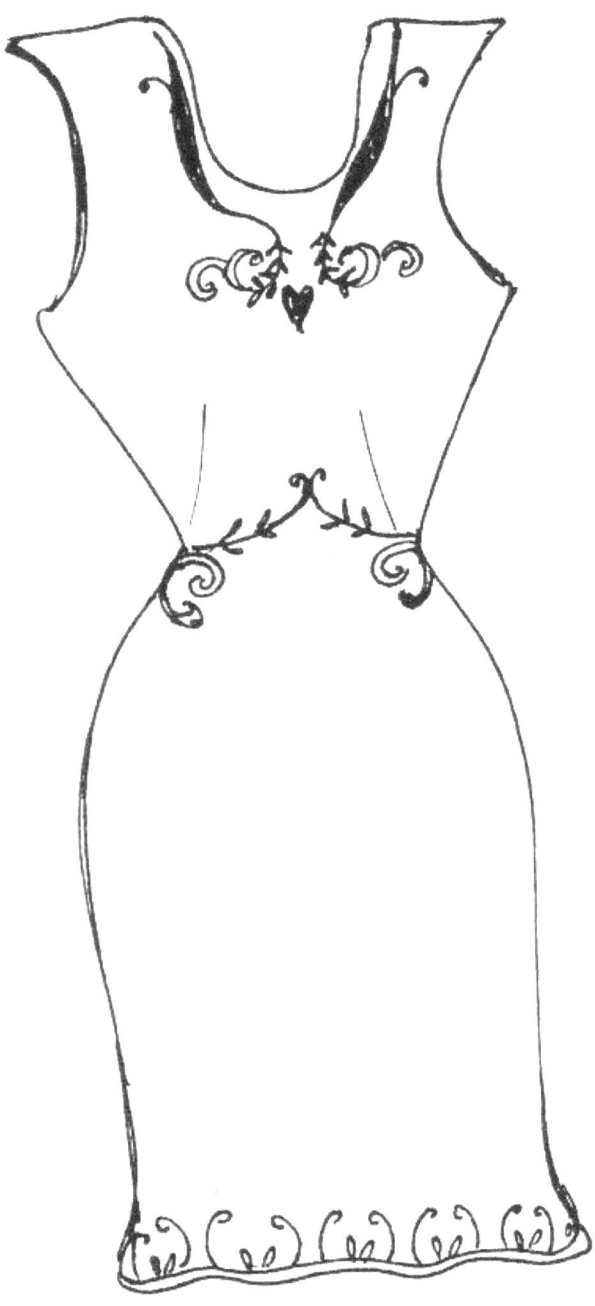

Bandany Apron

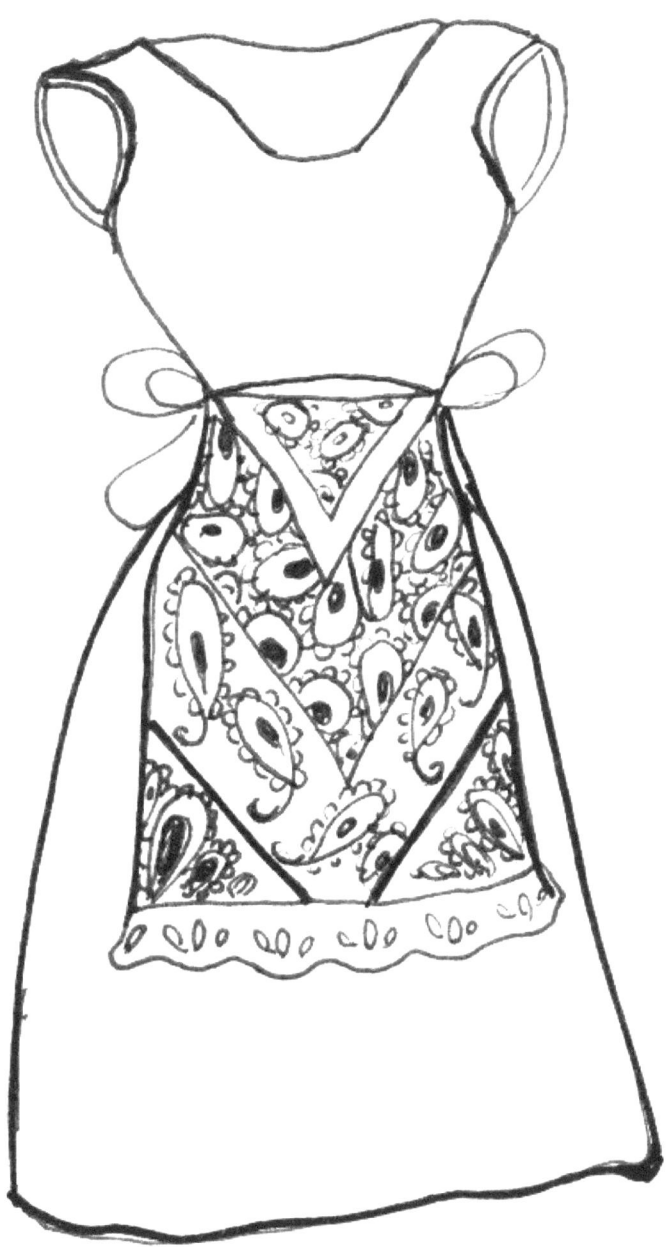

Western Classic

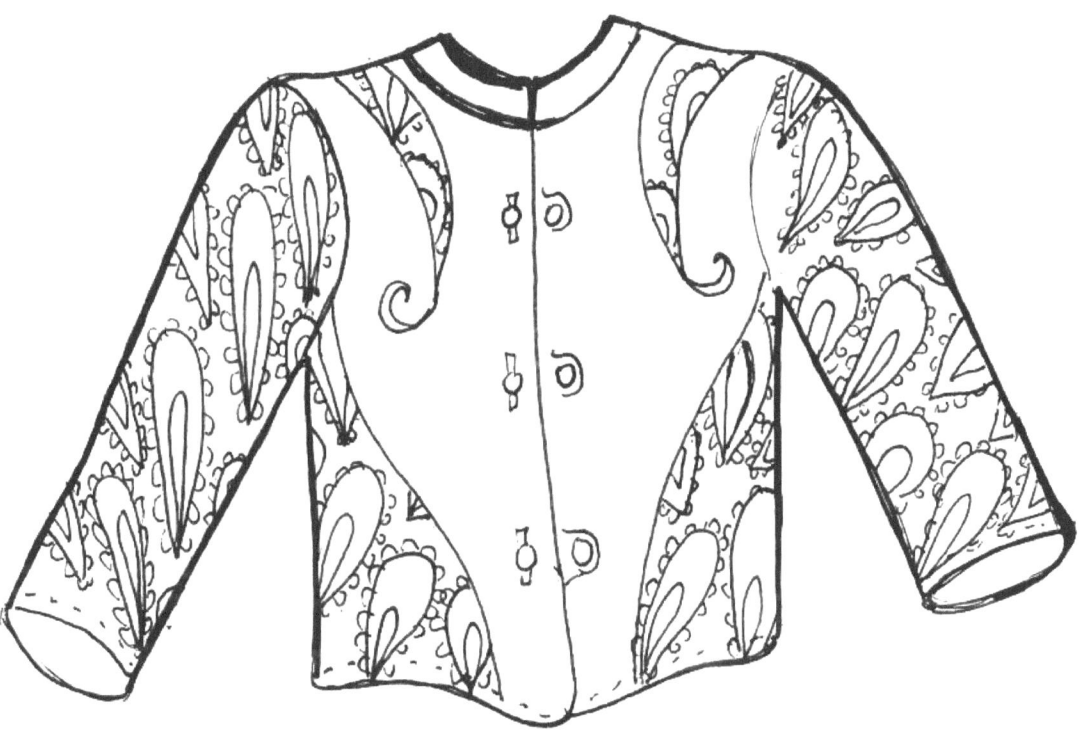

Cowgirl Flair

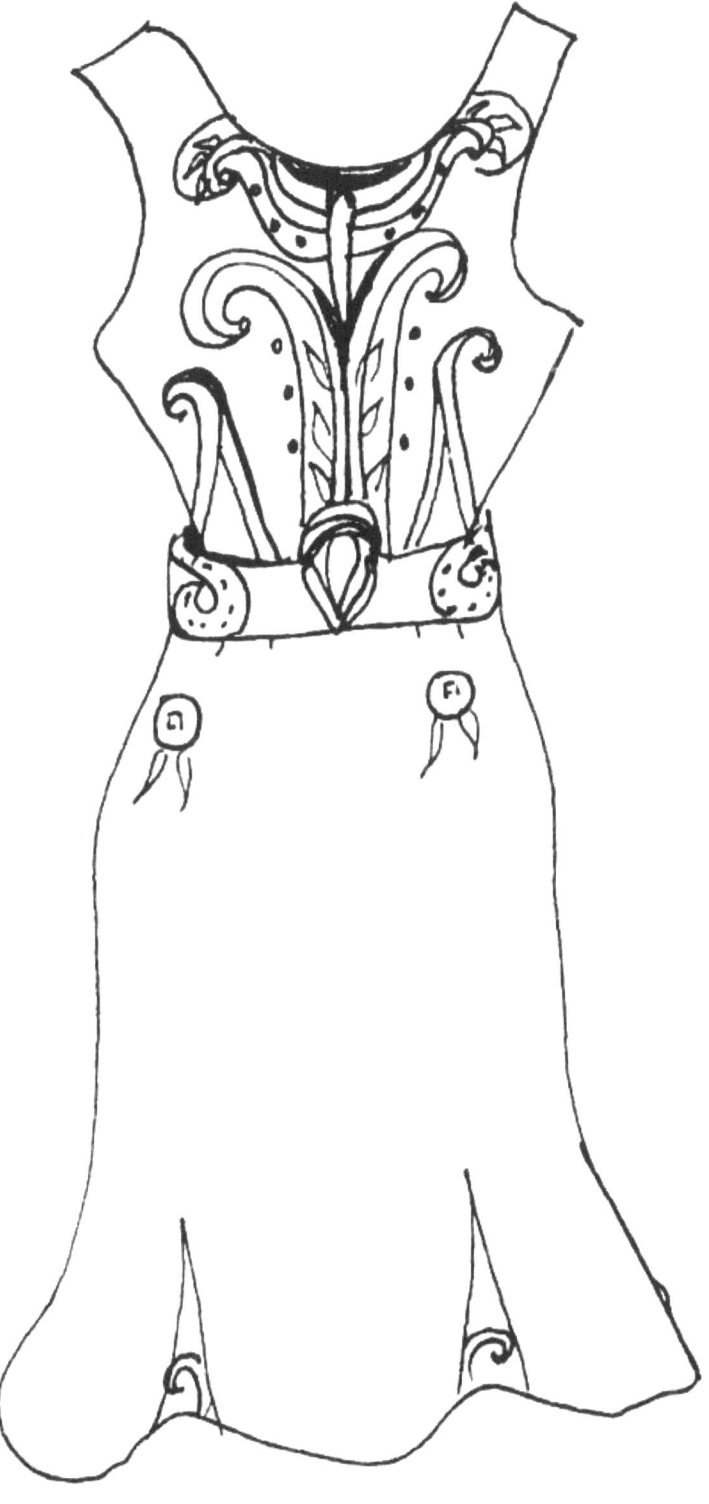

Bandany West

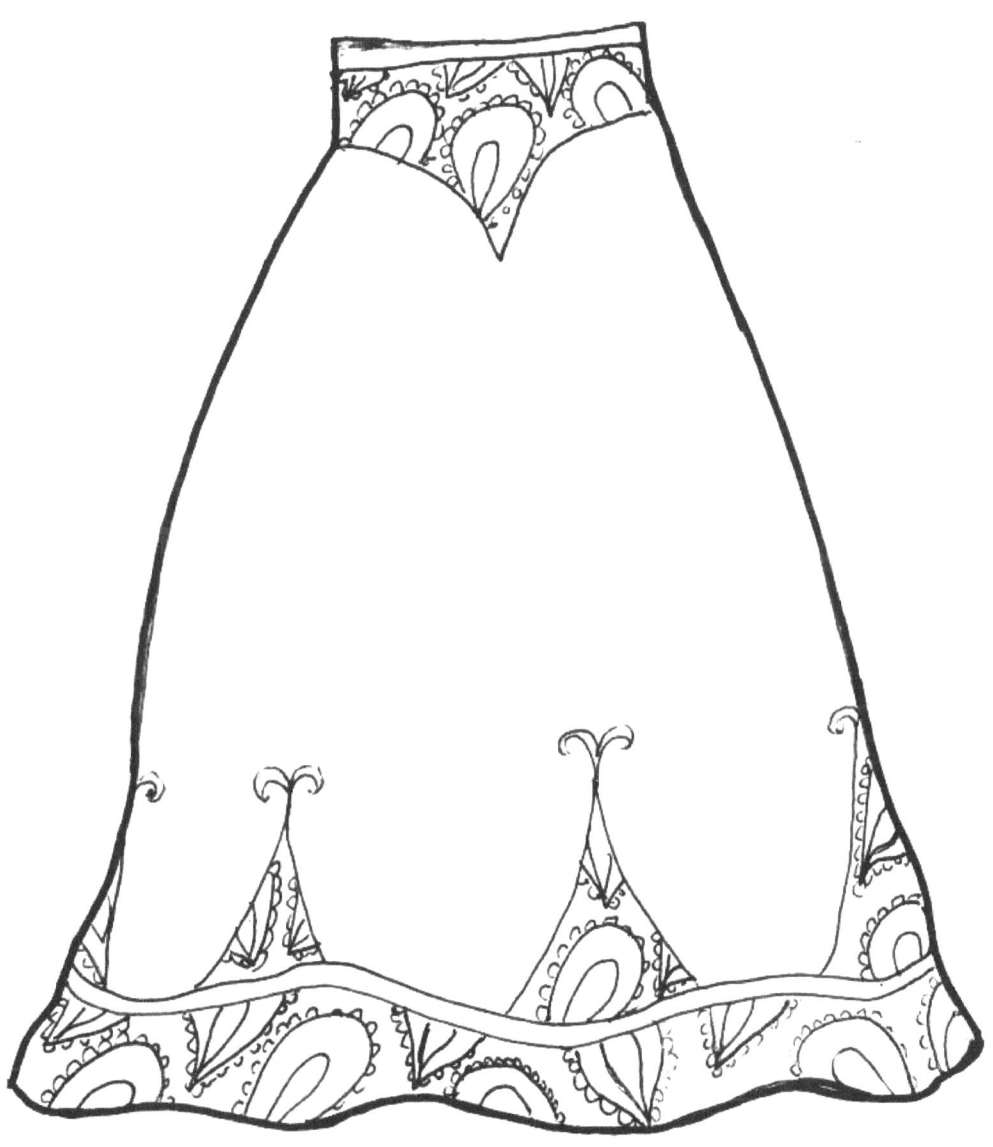

Up City Cowgirl

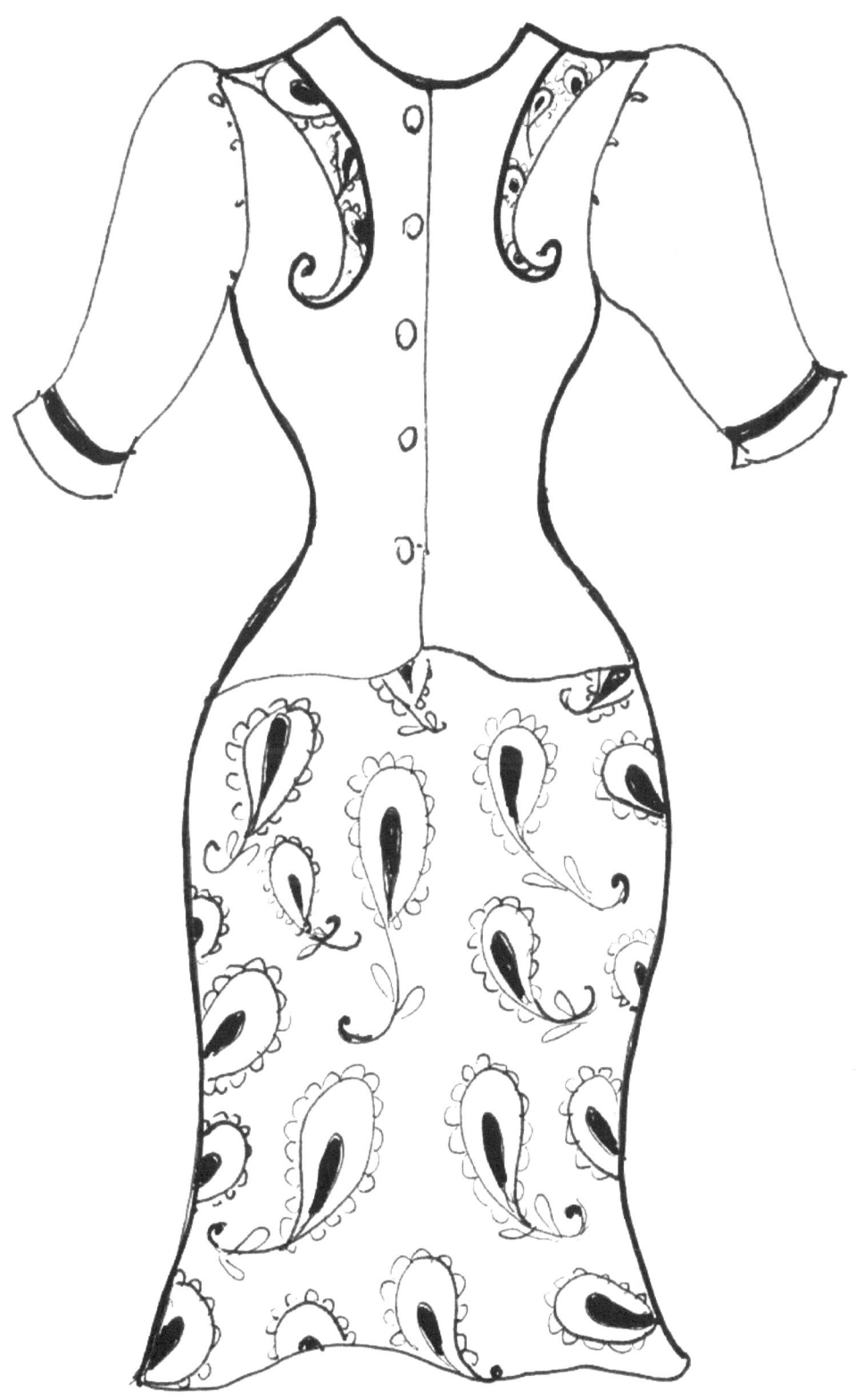

The Keeper

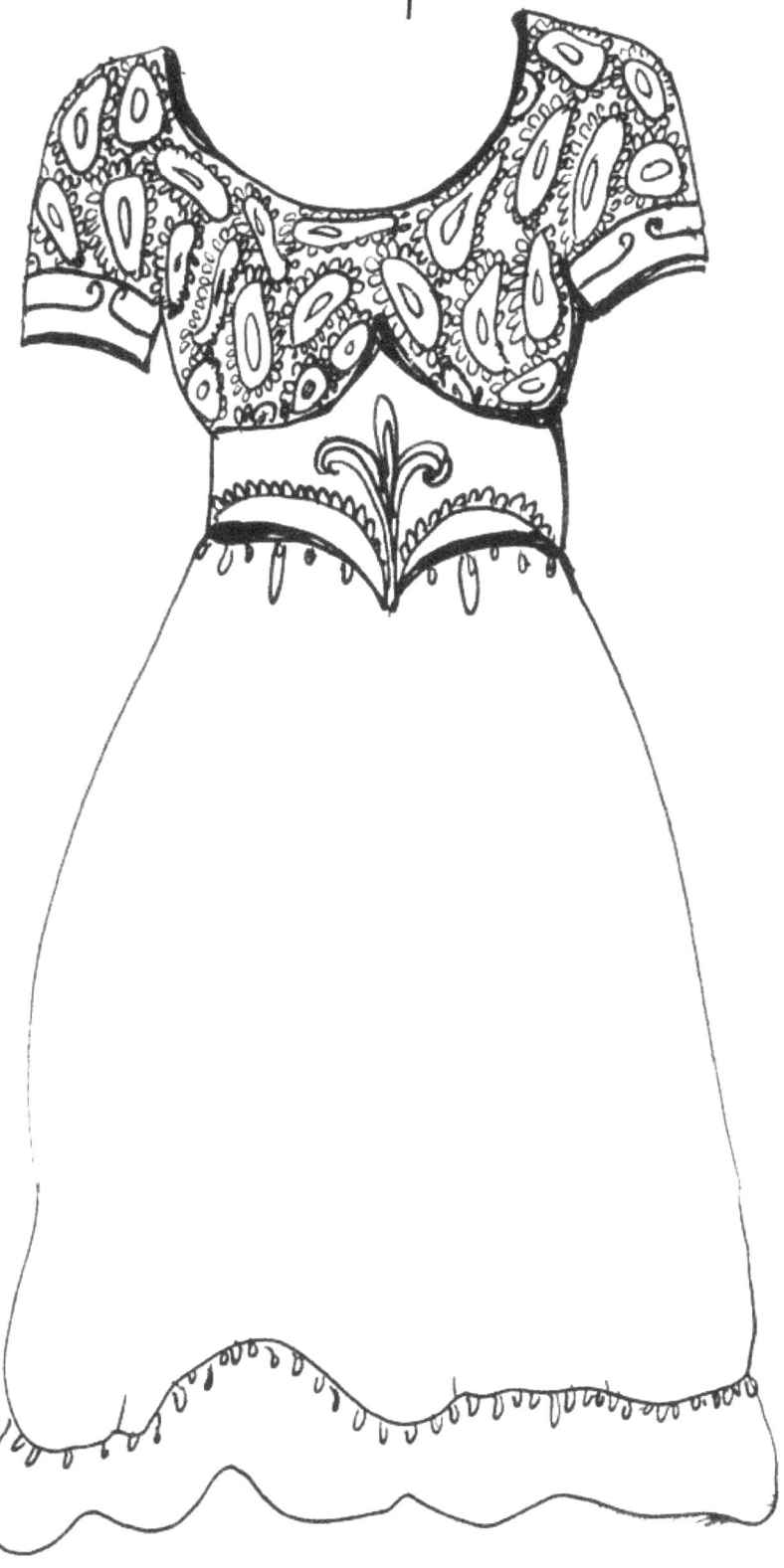

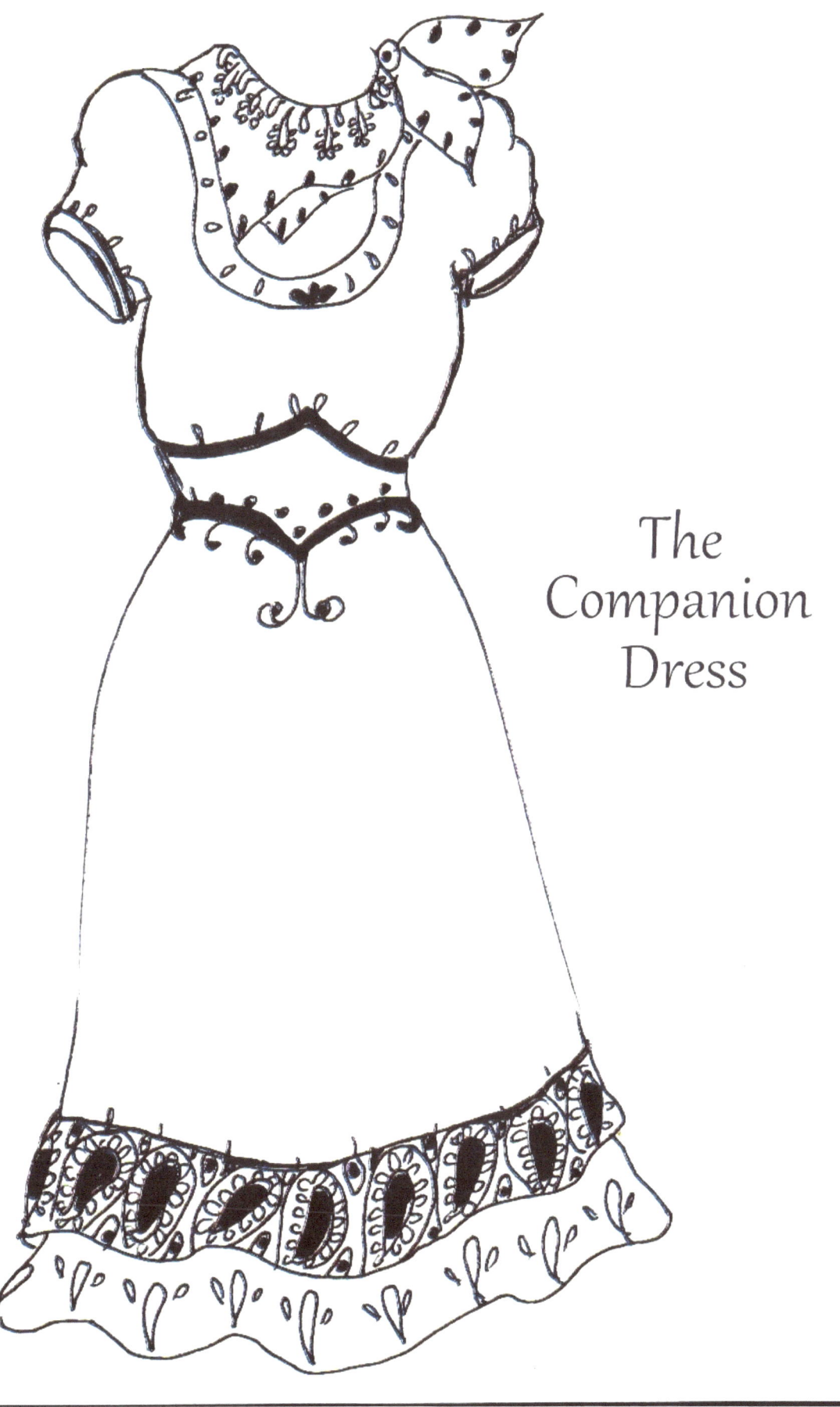

The
Companion
Dress

Pure Bandany

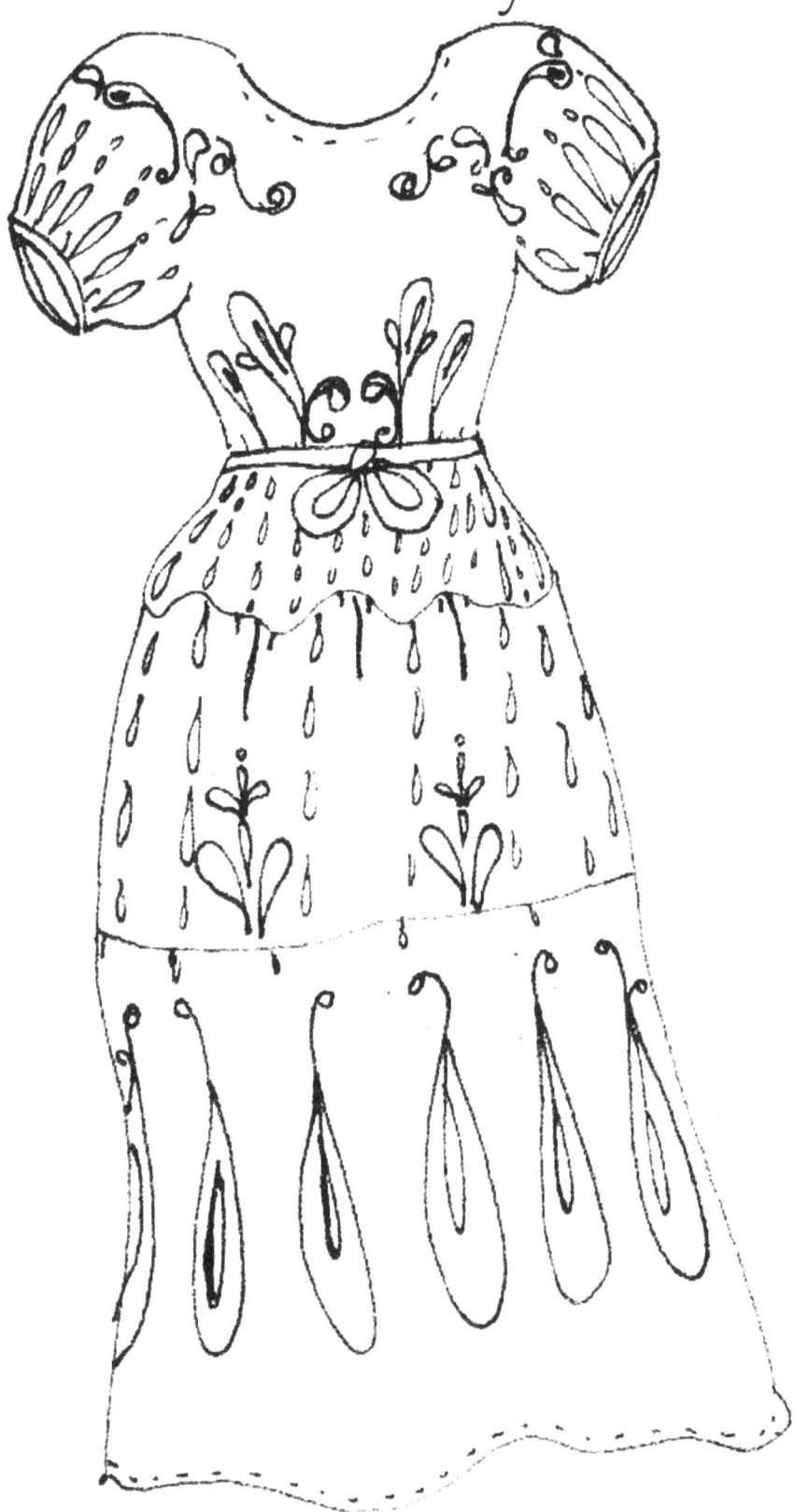

Cassandra Cloth

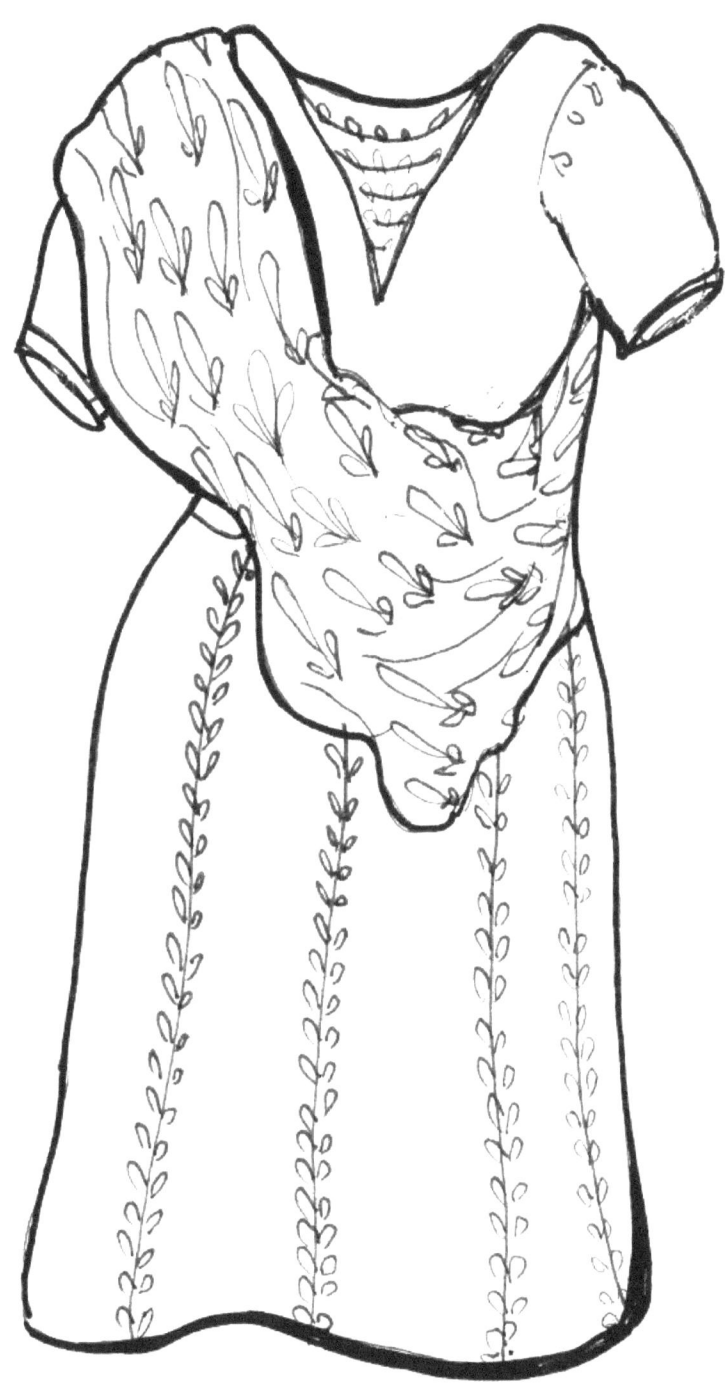

Bandany Mommy

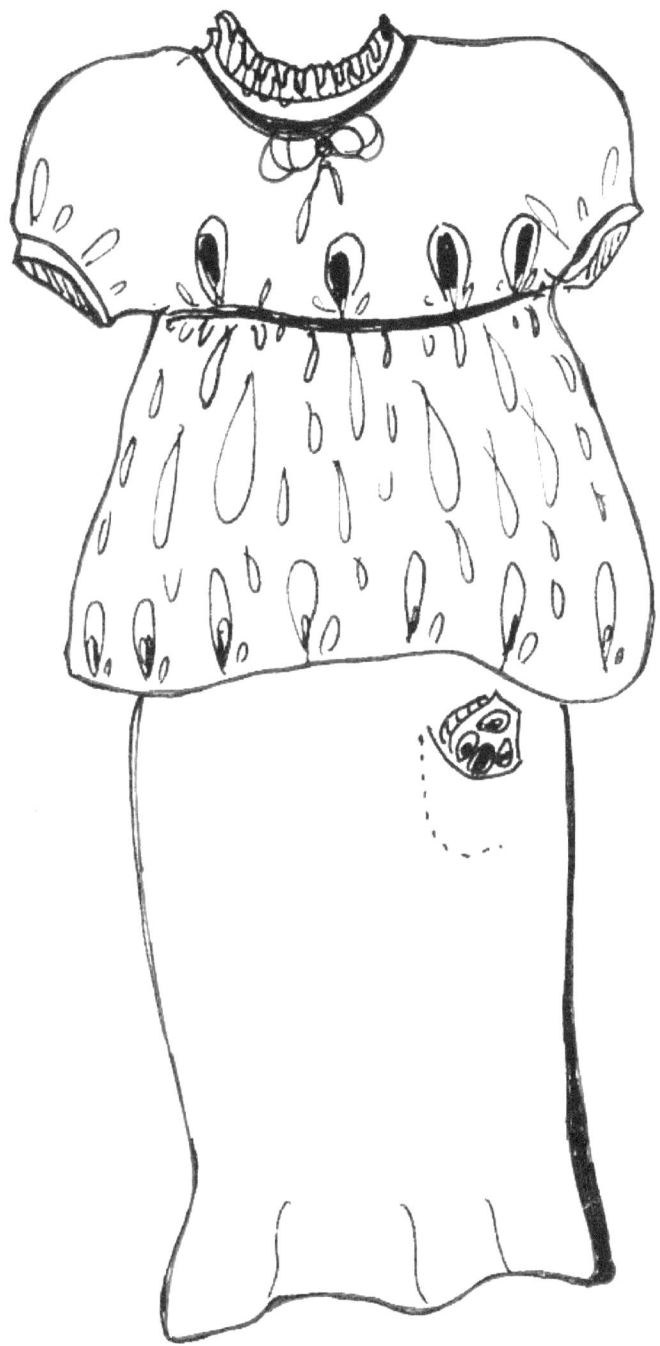

Classic Bandany

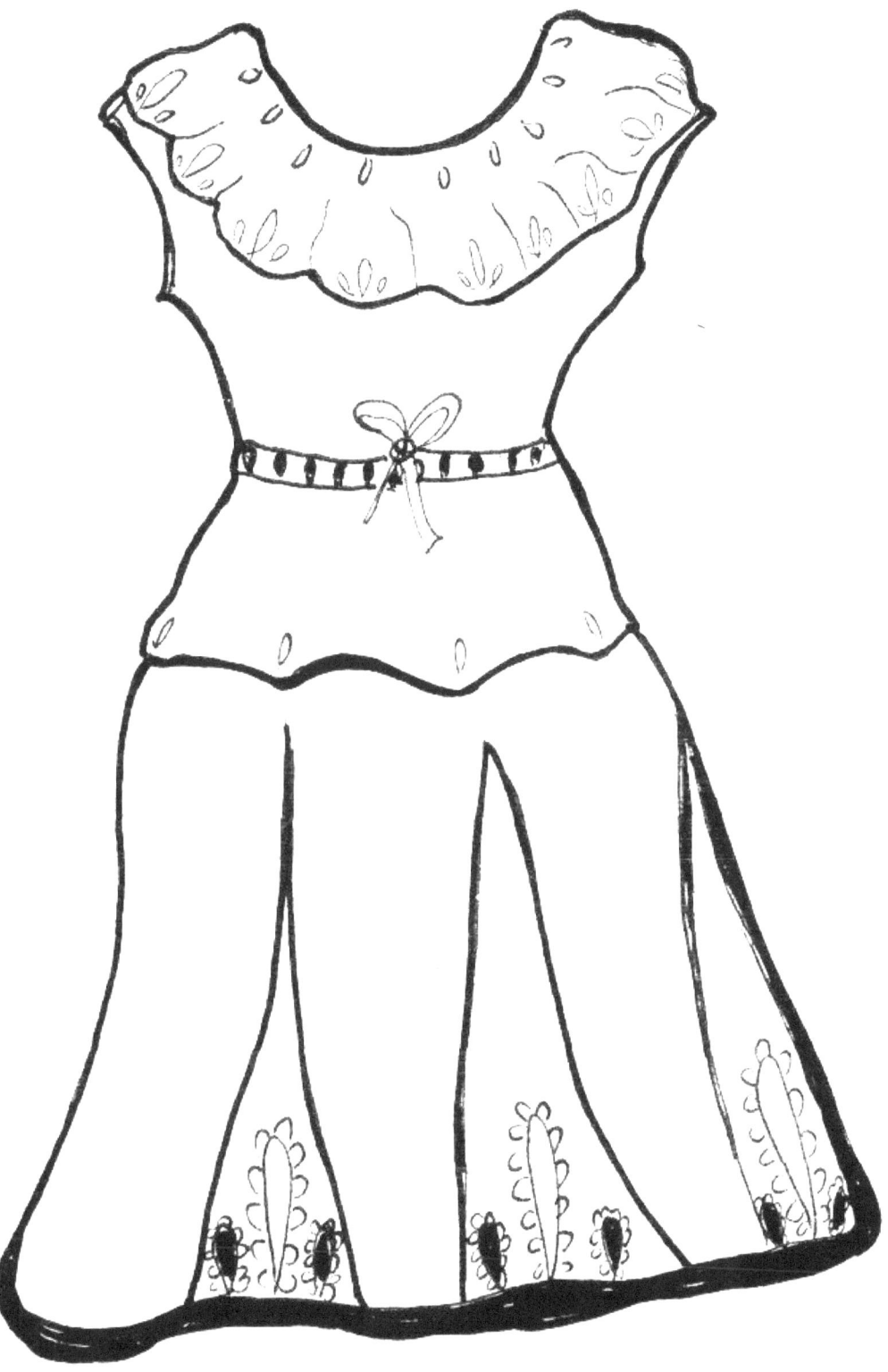

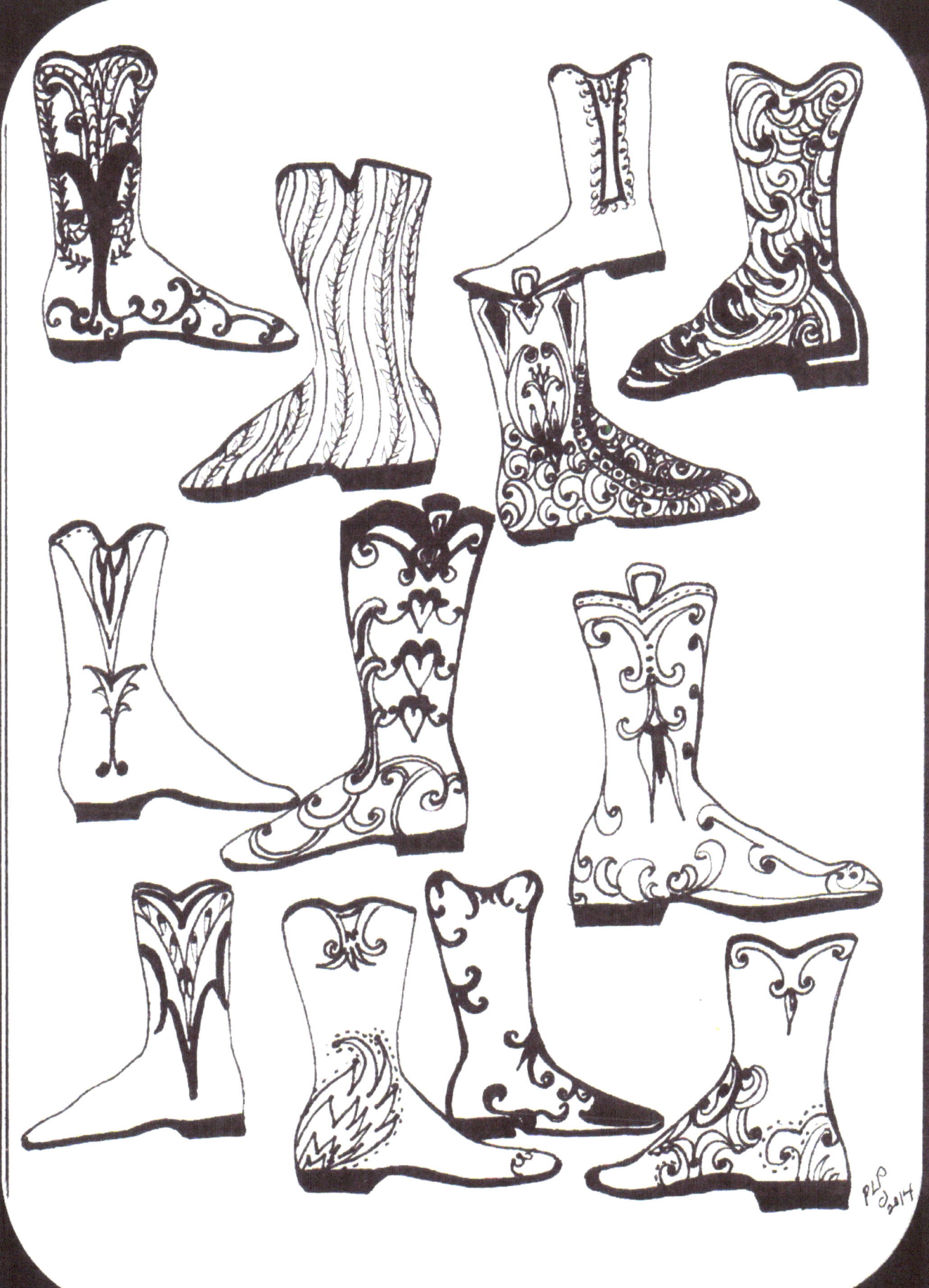

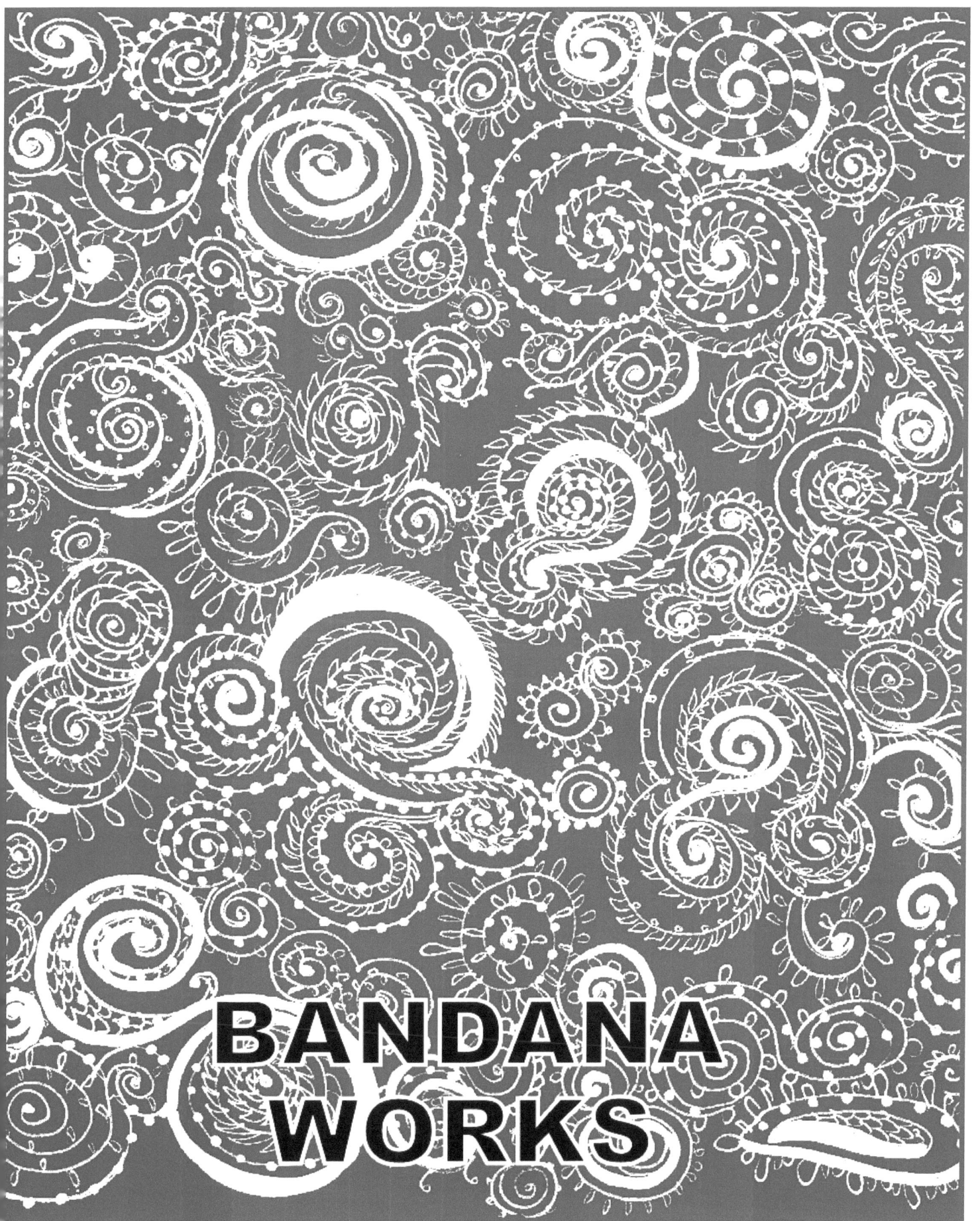

BANDANA
WORKS

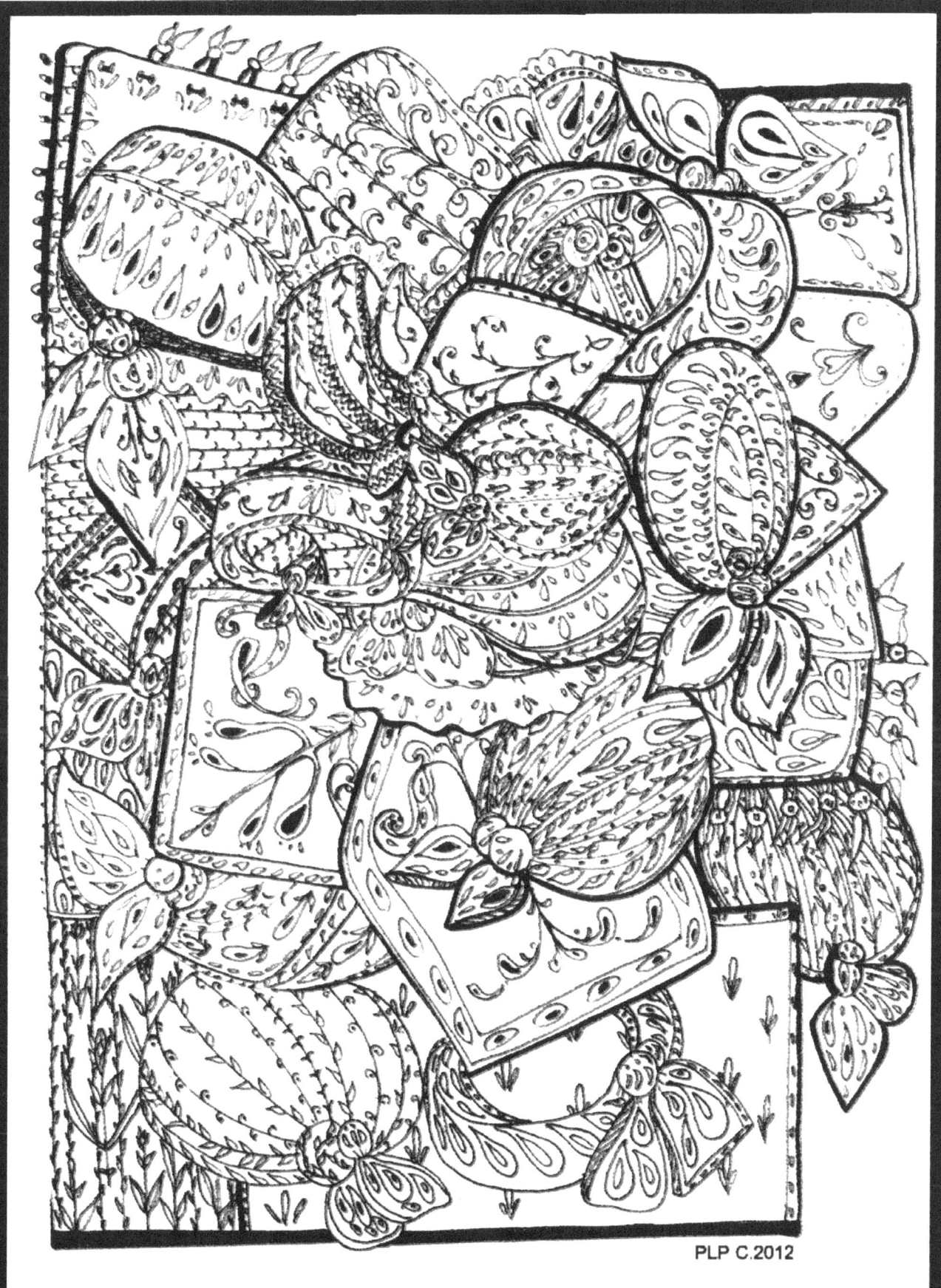

PLP C.2012

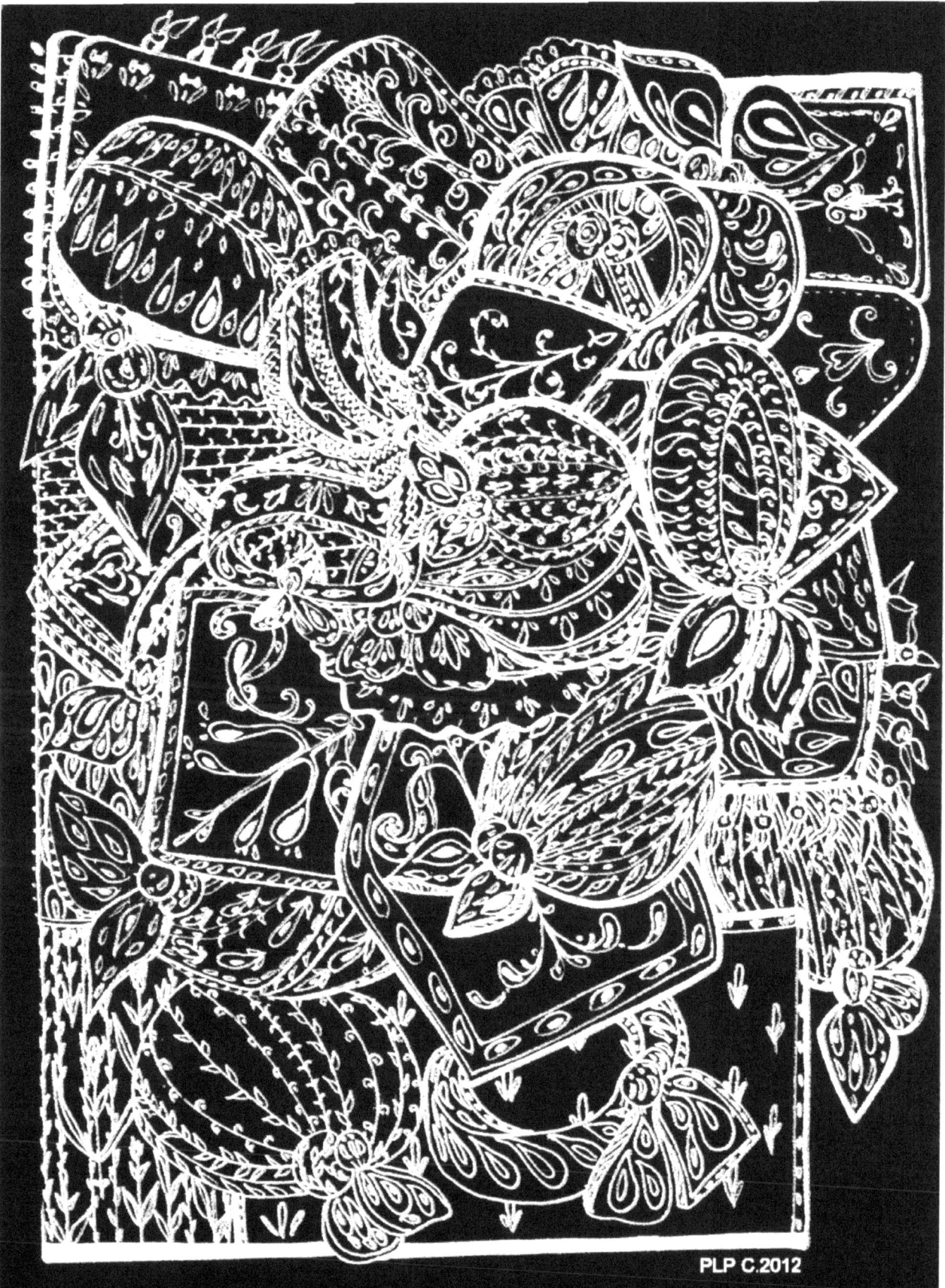

PLP C.2012

The artist and creator of this artistic work is Peggy Parrish. She lives in Parma , Idaho. Her hobbies of drawing and coloring have led her to doodle and draw several types of artwork. Her compilation over the years is being released in the form of Adult Coloring Books with a Bandana Theme. She also enjoys drawing the faces of Children from different ethnic backgrounds and fancy lettering. This work is only a small tip of the coloring "iceberg" she has to offer. She herself likes to sit and color to relax. Her hope is that you too will enjoy coloring and find great pleasure in doing so.

Peggy Louise Parrish

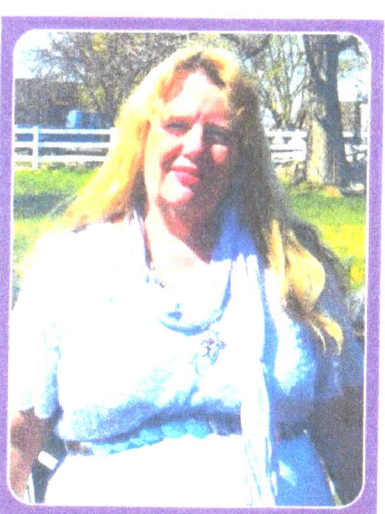

Keep watching for more Adult Coloring Books by this artist and author.

"MAY THE LORD BLESS THE WORKS OF MY HANDS AND YOURS"

www.ingramcontent.com/pod-product-compliance
Lightning Source LLC
Chambersburg PA
CBHW050746180526
45159CB00003B/1368